AUSTRALIA

by Madeline Donaldson

PULL AHEAD BOOKS
Continents

Lerner Publications Company • Minneapolis

Lerner Publications Company
A division of Lerner Publishing Group
241 First Avenue North
Minneapolis, MN 55401 U.S.A.

Website address: www.lernerbooks.com

Words in **bold type** are explained in a glossary on page 30.

Library of Congress Cataloging-in-Publication Data

Donaldson, Madeline.
    Australia / by Madeline Donaldson.
      p.   cm. − (Pull ahead books)
    Summary: Introduces the continent of Australia and some of its unique characteristics.
    Includes bibliographical references and index.
    ISBN-13: 978-0-8225-4718-1 (lib. bdg. : alk. paper)
    ISBN-10: 0-8225-4718-X (lib. bdg. : alk. paper)
    1. Australia—Juvenile literature. [1. Australia.] I. Title. II. Series.
    DU96.D66 2005
    994−dc21   2003023354

Manufactured in the United States of America
2 3 4 5 6 7 − JR − 12 11 10 09 08 07

Boing! Boing! Where could you watch
kangaroos jumping?

The **continent** of Australia!
A continent is a big piece of land.

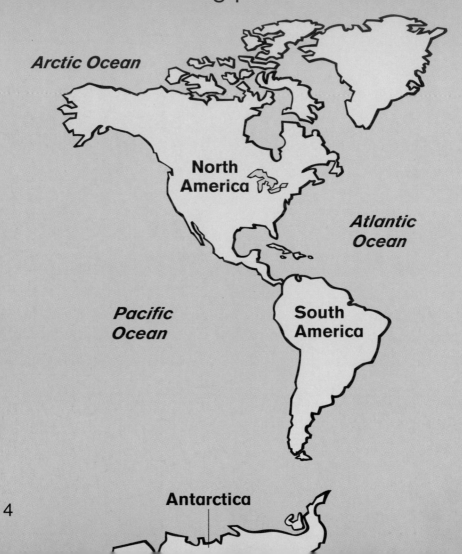

Arctic Ocean

North America

Atlantic Ocean

Pacific Ocean

South America

Antarctica

There are seven continents on Earth. Australia is the smallest.

Australia is the only continent that is also a **country**. Australia's **capital** city is Canberra.

The island of Tasmania is also part of Australia. This is a forest of eucalyptus trees on Tasmania.

Oceans surround Australia on all sides.

Surf's up! Australians swim and surf in the continent's ocean waters.

Off the northeastern coast of Australia
is the Great Barrier Reef. It is the
world's largest **coral reef**.

Animals called
corals live in the
warm waters
around the reef.

The highest parts of Australia are in the south and east.

Catch air! Australians enjoy skiing and snowboarding there in the winter.

Farmers grow wheat in the lowest parts of Australia. This land lies near the middle of the continent.

Deserts cover much of western
Australia. Watch out for snakes like
the desert death adder!

The grasslands of western Australia
feed huge herds of cattle and sheep.
These are merino sheep.

They are kicking
up dust as they go
into a paddock, or
holding area.

Remember the jumping kangaroos?

They are **marsupials.**
Marsupials raise their babies in pouches.

Platypuses are found only in Australia. They have a wide, flat nose called a snout.

Munch! Munch! This koala is eating the leaves of a eucalyptus tree.

Acacia trees are found all over
Australia. Some kinds of acacia trees
have bright flowers.

Most Australians live in large cities along the coasts. Sydney is the continent's biggest city.

One of Sydney's famous buildings is the **opera** house. Here, singers perform in musical plays called operas.

Few people live in the **outback**. This is the open countryside in the middle of Australia.

Zoom! Some people in the outback get around by airplane.

Australia has many interesting parts!
Do you know about Ayers Rock?
The **Aborigines**, or first Australians,
call the huge rock Uluru.

There's always something new to learn about Australia!

Cool Facts about Australia

- Australia covers almost 3 million square miles (8 million square kilometers).

- The animals of Australia include echidnas, kangaroos, koalas, kookaburras, platypuses, Tasmanian devils, and wallabies.

- Plants living in Australia include acacia (or wattle) trees, eucalyptus (or gum) trees, and grass trees.

- About 20 million people live in Australia. Nearly all of them speak English.

- Aborigines make up a very small part—only 1 percent—of Australia's 20 million people.

- The large cities of Australia are Sydney, Brisbane, Melbourne, Perth, and Adelaide. Canberra is the capital city.

Map of Australia

Indian Ocean

Pacific Ocean

Great Barrier Reef

Great Sandy Desert

O u t b a c k

C e n t r a l   L o w l a n d s

Brisbane

Great Victoria Desert

Adelaide

Perth

Sydney

Canberra

Melbourne

Indian Ocean

Tasmania

Glossary

Aborigines: a group of people who were the first to live in Australia

capital: a city where a government is based

continent: one of seven big pieces of land on Earth

coral reef: an area of coral rocks that lies near the surface of water. Coral rocks are the skeletons of once-living animals called corals.

country: a place where people live and share the same laws

marsupials: animals whose females carry their babies in a pouch on the mother's stomach

opera: a play set to music and sung by singers

outback: the open countryside of central Australia

Further Reading and Website

Arnold, Caroline. *Australian Animals.* New York: HarperCollins, 2000.

Brode, Robyn. *Bush Pilot! Flying High over Australia.* Hauppauge, NY: Barron's, 2002.

Davis, Kevin A. *Look What Came from Australia.* New York: Franklin Watts, 1999.

Foster, Leila Merrell. *Australia.* Crystal Lake, IL: Heinemann Library, 2002.

Fowler, Allan. *Australia.* New York: Children's Press, 2001.

Germein, Katrina. *Big Rain Coming.* Boston: Houghton Mifflin, 2000.

McCollum, Sean. *Australia.* Minneapolis: Carolrhoda Books, Inc., 1999.

Nelson, Robin. *Where Is My Continent?* Minneapolis: Lerner Publications Company, 2002.

Olawsky, Lynn Ainsworth. *Colors of Australia.* Minneapolis: Carolrhoda Books, Inc., 1997.

Sayre, April Pulley. *G'Day Australia!* Brookfield, CT: Millbrook Press, 2003.

Enchanted Learning

http://enchantedlearning.com/geography/australia

The geography section of this website has links to every continent.

Index